To Ivor

Been **SHAFTED** by a man?

BURY yourself in laughter

How to Shaft a Shafter

SHAFTES-BURY MAN

Kay Allen

ISBN 095470590 - 4

Executive Editor Kay Allen
Designed and Produced by Livewire Intelligent Media Ltd
Published by Diverse Advice Limited
Cartoon illustrations by Dave Ball.
www.car-toonshop.co.uk
www.shaftesburyman.com

This edition is published by
Diverse Advice Limited 10 Woodman Court Shaftesbury Dorset SP7 8PY

CONTENTS

It may look like a man, but it is not!

This is Shaftesbury Man, a primitive specimen which dates back to Neanderthal Man. This book is filled with essential information on his habitat, feeding habits, mating rituals, occupations and recreation. It gives an insight into his intelligence and offers women advice and guidance on living with Shaftesbury Man.

Men are from Mars

Women are from Venus

Shaftesbury Man is from Uranus

Habitat

Shaftesbury Man's natural habitat is a secure enclosure called 'The Pub'. Here Shaftesbury Man can bond with other Shaftesbury Men and swap stories about their day.

How many Shaftesbury Men does it take to change a light bulb?

5 – One to change the bulb and the rest to meet him in the football club to listen to him moan about what a hard day he has had!

As Shaftesbury Man has little imagination the bar maid obliges and wears clothes that leave nothing to the imagination!

The pub provides the opportunity to practice his mating calls to the female of the species such as:

"Get on all fours and shake 'em!"

*The pub also provides Shaftesbury man with the source of his wit, humour and intelligence! - **Lager***

Watering Holes

Shaftesbury Man requires a minimum of 15 pints of lager which must be consumed at high speed whilst he still remains vertical.

Vertical Binge drinking is an essential skill for the survival of Shaftesbury Man.

Shaftesbury Man's ability to communicate to woman is inversely proportionate to the amount of lager consumed.

Man must believe in something

Shaftesbury Man believes that lager solves all problems.

Shaftesbury Man's IQ is inversely proportionate to the amount of lager consumed

The Journey Home

Leaving the safety of their natural habitat can be dangerous

The escape requires cunning!

The local constabulary heard Shaftesbury Man had a heavy session in the Football Club. A policeman waited outside ready to outwit his prey.

At closing time as everyone came out, he spotted his potential quarry. Dicky was so obviously inebriated that he could barely walk. He stumbled around the car park for a few minutes, looking for his car. After trying his keys on five others, he finally found his own vehicle. He sat in the car a good ten minutes as the other Shaftesbury Men drove off. He turned his lights on, then off, wipers on then off. He started to pull forward into the grass, and then stopped. Finally, when he was the last car, he pulled out onto the road and started to drive away.

The eager policeman pulled Dicky over. He administered the Breathalyser test, and to his great surprise the man blew a 0.00!

The policeman was dumbfounded!
"This equipment must be broken!" exclaimed the policeman

"*I doubt it,*" said Dicky. *"Tonight I'm the Designated Decoy!"*

He went that way officer

The journey home is fraught with dangers and unexpected difficulties. 15 pints of lager can make remembering which is his lair confusing

What are you doing trying to get into that house, you live here!

Shaftesbury Man is not drunk if he can still hold on to
the ground and not fall off

*Sometimes Shaftesbury man doesn't make it home at
all - but his survival instincts are strong and he can
sleep anywhere*

On his way home Shaftesbury Man is required to be the hunter-gatherer and bring home the food

The return home from the pub requires Shaftesbury Man to summon all his wit and intellect!

Shaftesbury Man was not home at his usual hour, and the wife was fuming, as the clock ticked later and later. Finally, about 3:00 AM she heard a noise at the front door, and as she stood at the top of the stairs, there was her Shaftesbury Man, drunk as a skunk, trying to navigate the stairs. "Do you realise what time it is?" she said.

Shaftesbury Man thought about this and replied, "Don't get excited, I'm late because I bought something for the house." Immediately her attitude changed, and as she ran down the stairs to meet him halfway, she said, "What did you buy for the house, dear?"

His answer "A round of drinks!"

Shaftesbury Man had been enjoying the sanctity of his natural habitat all day so he decided he had better go home so as not to piss off the wife by drinking after work.

When he gets home he sneaks upstairs quietly only to find her in bed with another man.

Later, back in the pub, he was telling his 5 Shaftesbury mates. "That's awful," they said. "What did you do?"

"Well, I sneaked back out real quiet – I mean, they had only just started so I figured I had time for a couple more pints!!"

Occupations

The Amateur Farmer

The Shaftesbury Farmer and his wife are in bed. He reaches forward and feels her breasts. He says, "You know, if these were bigger we wouldn't need the cow."

She reaches back to feel his penis and says, "If this was bigger we wouldn't need the farm manager."

Whilst at work Shaftesbury Farmer crashed his tractor into a prize garden, spilling 100 tonnes of slurry.
Instead of apologising to the horrified housedholder, he asked for payment for the fertilizer.

That'll do wonders for your Roses love!

The Truck Driver

The Shaftesbury Truck Driver was eating in a cafe when three Hell's Angels bikers walked in. The first walked up to Shaftesbury Man, pushed his cigarette into his pie and then took a seat at the counter.

The second walked up to Shaftesbury Man, spat into his coffee and took a seat at the counter. The third walked up to Shaftesbury Man, turned over his plate, and then he took a seat at the counter with his buddies.

Without a word of protest, the Shaftesbury Man quietly paid his bill and left the cafe. One of the bikers said to the waitress, "Humph, not much of a man was he?" Shaking her head, she replied, "No . . . not much of a truck driver either."

He had just backed his truck over three motorcycles.

The Roofer

Shaftesbury Roofer chose his profession because people kept telling him that there were free drinks on the house.

The GroundWorker

Shaftesbury Man was working so hard on a building site carrying bricks up the ladder that his mate got worried. *"What's up with you, working so hard?"* he asked. *"Don't worry,"* said the other. *"I've got them all fooled. It's the same load of bricks each time."*

The Coach Driver

As the coach driver was driving down the M1, his phone rang. Answering, he heard his mum's voice urgently warning him, *"Ivor, I just heard on the news that some idiot is driving the wrong way on the M1."*

"Hell," said Ivor, *"It's not just one car. It's hundreds of them!"*

IVOR the COACHDRIVER likes to show off his driving to the ladies.

Recreation

Shooting

Two Shaftesbury Men were out shooting ducks. One took aim and hit a bird which tumbled out of the sky to land at his feet. "Ah, you should have saved the bullet," said the other. "The fall would have killed him, anyway."

Two Shaftesbury Men were out duck-shooting. They had their guns and dogs and walked for hours with no success. Dropping into the pub on the way back they listened with envy to all the other Guns who had obviously been very successful. "Where do you think we went wrong?" asked one. His friend thought for a minute. "You know, I think it must be that we're not throwing the dogs high enough."

Horse Racing

A woman came up behind her Shaftesbury Man while he was enjoying his morning tea and whacked him on the back of the head. "I found a piece of paper in your back pocket with the name 'Shagable girl' written on it," she said, furious. "You had better have a damn good explanation."

"Honey, please calm down!" Shaftesbury Man replied. *"Remember last week when I was at the races? That was the name of the horse I bet on."*

The next morning, his wife snuck up on him and whacked him again. *"What was that for?"* he complained.

"Your horse called last night!!"

Digging Holes

Two farmers were competing for a contract to put up telegraph poles. The authorities decided to test them, seeing which farmer could put up the most poles in an hour. The first farmer achieved twenty but Shaftesbury Farmer managed only two.

"I'm afraid you lost the job," Shaftesbury Man was told. "The other boys managed twenty to your two."

"Ah," came the reply, "but he cheated. Did you see how much he left sticking out of the ground?"

A Shaftesbury Man was digging a hole in a road when a passer-by asked him what he was going to do with all the soil.

"Ah, well," he replied, " I'll dig another hole."
"But what if it doesn't all fit in?"

"Oh, I've thought of that," said the man. "I'll dig the next hole deeper."

There were two Shaftesbury Men working for Denny's Construction. One would dig holes in the ground and the other would come behind him and fill in the holes. "Tell me," said the passer-by, "What on earth are you doing?"

"Well," said the digger," Usually there are three of us. I dig, Tommy plants the tree and Mick fills in the hole. Today Tommy is off ill, but that doesn't mean Mick and I get the day off, does it?"

Shaftesbury Man has prowess in the bedroom

Di and Shaz meet to discuss their close encounters with Shaftesbury Man. They begin to talk and bring each other up to date. The conversation covers their work, hobbies, homes, etc., and finally gets around to their sex lives.

Shaz said, "It's okay. We get it on every week or so but it's no big adventure. How's yours?"

Di replied, "It's just great, ever since we got into S & M." Sharon is aghast. "Really, Di, I never would have guessed that you would go for that sort of thing."

"Oh, sure," says Di, "He snores while I masturbate."

One Shaftesbury Man asks the other, "Hey, have you ever gone to bed with an ugly woman?"

The second man says, "No, but I've woken up with plenty."

What's a Shaftesbury Man's idea of honesty in a relationship?

Telling you his real name.

Shaftesbury Man has great - solving ability

A Shaftesbury Man walked into a therapist's office looking very depressed. "Doc, you've got to help me. I can't go on like this."

"What's the problem?" the doctor inquired.

"Well, I'm 35 years old and I still have no luck with the ladies. No matter how hard I try, I just seem to scare them away," replied the man.

The doctor said, "My friend, this is not a serious problem. You just need to work on your self-esteem. Each morning, I want you to get up and run to the bathroom mirror. Tell yourself that you are a good person, a fun person, and an attractive person. But say it with real conviction. Within a week you'll have women buzzing all around you."

The man seemed content with this advice and walked out of the office a bit excited. Three weeks later he returned with the same downtrodden expression on his face.

"Did my advice not work?" asked the doctor.

"It worked all right. For the past several weeks I've enjoyed some of the best moments in my life with the most fabulous looking women."

"So, what is your problem?" asked the doctor. "I don't have a problem," the man replied. "My wife does."

Shaftesbury Man has superb knowledge of the female form

A couple of Shaftesbury Men who had been without sex for several weeks, decided that they needed to visit a local brothel.

When they arrived, the madam took one look at them and decided she wasn't going to waste any of her girls on these two drunken men. Figuring on Shaftesbury Man's lack of intelligence she used "blow-up" dolls instead. She put a doll in each of the men's room and left them to their business.

After the two men were finished, they started for home and got to talking. The first man said, "I think the girl I had was dead. She never moved, talked or even groaned. How was it for you?"

The second man replied, "I think mine was a witch." The first man asked, "How's that?"

"Well," said the second man, "when I nibbled on her breast, she farted and flew out the window!"

Shaftesbury Man is adept at story-telling ability

A woman is in bed with her lover who also happens to be her Shaftesbury Man's best friend. They make love for hours, and afterwards, while they're just laying there, the phone rings.

Since it is the woman's house, she picks up the receiver. Her lover looks over at her and listens, only hearing her side of the conversation.

Speaking in a cheery voice, the woman says, "Hello? Oh, hi. I'm so glad that you called. Really? That's wonderful. I am so happy for you. That sounds terrific. Great! Thanks. Okay. Bye bye."

She hangs up the telephone and her lover asks, "Who was that?"

"Oh," she replies, "that was just my Shaftesbury Man telling me all about the wonderful time he's having shooting with you."

Shaftesbury Man has enormous powers of persuasion

Once upon a time, in a land far away, a beautiful, independent, self-assured princess happened upon a frog as she sat contemplating ecological issues on the shores of an unpolluted pond in a verdant meadow near her castle.

The frog hopped into the princess's lap and said: "Elegant Lady, I was once a handsome Shaftesbury Man, until an evil witch cast a spell upon me.

One kiss from you, however, and I will turn back into the dapper, young prince that I am and then, my sweet, we can marry and set up housekeeping in yon castle with my mother, where you can prepare my meals, clean my clothes, bear my children, and forever feel grateful and happy doing so."

That night, on a repast of lightly sautéed frogs legs seasoned in a white wine and onion cream sauce, she chuckled to herself and thought:

"I don't fucking think so..."

Shaftesbury Man has a way with words

Sorry I didn't call home angel – I have had such a 'hard' day you would not believe it!

Employee relations

Trev feels a bit hung over one morning so he rings his boss and pulls a sicky. "I am really sick boss and can't work today."

Ivor says, "You know what I do Trev when I feel ill. I go to my wife and ask her for a blow job – makes me feel better every time. You should try that."

Two hours later Trev calls Ivor, "Boss, I did what you said and you are right, I feel great, I'll be in work soon. By the way your wife says don't forget to pick up the dry cleaning!!!"

Intelligence

It is important to gain an insight into Shaftesbury Man's intellect - never attribute to malice what can be explained by stupidity

How do you make Shaftesbury Man's eyes light up?
Shine a torch in his ears

What happened to the Shaftesbury Man who ate a fly?
He had more brains in his stomach

What do you get if you offer Shaftesbury Man a penny for his thoughts?
Change!

What do you call an intelligent, sober Shaftesbury Man?
A myth!

What's the difference between Bigfoot and an intelligent Shaftesbury Man?
> *Bigfoot has been spotted several times*

What do you say to Shaftesbury Man after Sex?
> *Anything - he's asleep*

What is Shaftesbury Man's idea of multi-tasking?
> *Drinking, burping and farting at the same time*

Scientists have discovered intelligent DNA in some Shaftesbury Men
> *Unfortunately, 95% of them shot it out!*

Shaftesbury Man tries to fool all of the people some of the time and some of the people all of the time – but he can't fool his mum!

Advice to women

FOR WOMEN WHO MUST LIVE WITH SHAFTESBURY MAN - REMEMBER

1. Don't imagine you can change a Shaftesbury Man.
   Unless he's still in nappies.

2. If your Shaftesbury Man walks out.
   Shut the door quick and change the locks.

3. Never let your Shaftesbury Man's mind wander.
   It's too little to be out alone.

4. Go for younger Shaftesbury Men.
   They never mature anyway.

5. Shaftesbury Men are all the same.
   They just have different faces so that you can tell them apart.

6. Women don't make fools of Shaftesbury Men.
   Most of them are the do-it-yourself types.

7. Sadly, all Shaftesbury Men are created equal.

Remember what happened to the woman who advertised for a husband in Shaftesbury?

she got a 100 offers all saying "take mine"

CONVERSATIONS WITH WOMEN WHO LIVE WITH SHAFTESBURY MAN

Two women discussing Shaftesbury Man
> First woman: *My fantasy is to have two blokes at once.*

> Second woman: *Me too! One for the cleaning and one for the cooking!*

Two women are having a conversation about their Shaftesbury Men when the first one says, "My bloke said he fantasised about having two girls at once." The other replied, "Yeah, most blokes do - what did you tell him?"

I said, "If you can't satisfy one woman why would you want to piss off two?"

My Shaftesbury Man is an Angel
> *You're lucky - mine is still alive*

Why doesn't Shaftesbury Man ever go through the male menopause?
He never gets past puberty.

Why do Shaftesbury Men name their penises?
Because they want to be on a first-name basis with the one who makes all their decisions.

What does a clitoris, an anniversary, and a toilet have in common?
Shaftesbury Men always miss them.

What's the difference between a new Shaftesbury Man and a new dog?
After a year, the dog is still excited to see you.

What makes Shaftesbury Men chase women they have no intention of marrying?
The same urge that makes dogs chase cars they have no intention of driving.

Shaftesbury Man said to his girlfriend – "why don't you tell me when you have an orgasm?"
She said – "I would but you are never there!"

Shaftesbury Man was feeling unwell and complaining that he could not do all the things he was used to. He decided to visit the doctor.

When the examination is complete, the Shaftesbury Man says, "Tell me in plain English doc, what's wrong with me?"

"Well, in plain English, you're just lazy and spending too much time in the pub," replies the doctor.

"OK," says Shaftesbury Man. "Now give me the medical term in Latin so I can fool the wife!"

Why do Shaftesbury Men become smarter during sex?
Because they are plugged into a genius

Why don't women blink during foreplay with a Shaftesbury Man?
They don't have enough time

Why do Shaftesbury Men snore when they lie on their backs?
Because their balls fall over their assholes and they vapour lock

An angry wife met her Shaftesbury Man at the door. There was alcohol on his breath and lipstick on his collar.

"I assume," she snarled, "that you have a bloody good reason for waltzing home at six in the morning?"

"Yep .....Breakfast!" he replied.

The Ultimate Shaftesbury Man Test

Is your man a Shaftesbury Man? Tick the answer that most applies to your man – then add up your score.

You spend ages getting ready for a night out with your man. Does he:

a) Say you look hot baby ☐

b) Not say anything ☐

c) Not turn up – he is in the pub with his mates ☐

If he goes shopping for food, does he:

a) Buy everything you needed ☐

b) Buy only food he likes ☐

c) Go to the pub and come home with a takeaway ☐

During a night of passion you produce a vibrator. Does he:

a) Say fantastic I love to turn you on

b) Not know what to do with it

c) Get cross because it means
        he has to do some work

If he farts in bed, does he:

a) Apologise

b) Ignore it

c) Laugh out loud and pull the bed covers
        over your head

After sex, does he:

a) Hold you tenderly ☐

b) Recover and want more ☐

c) Turn over and fall asleep ☐

Is your man's idea of romance:

a) An afternoon of lovemaking ☐

b) A night of passion ☐

c) A night away with his mates in Blackpool ☐

If his mate is having an affair, does he:

a) Refuse to speak to him ☐

b) Encourage him to end it ☐

c) Offer him a lift and cover for him ☐

Does he find tractors and diggers:

a) Boring ☐

b) Useful occasionally ☐

c) Fascinating and a source of conversation ☐

a   scores   1 point

b   scores   5 points

c   scores   10 points

If your man scored 10 and below

Your fella is a new man probably just outside the gene pool of Shaftesbury Man – keep hold of him tight and keep him away from Shaftesbury Woman

If your man scored 11 – 30

Your fella probably has some of the Shaftesbury Man gene pool. Your man is secure in himself, attentive and loving but beware of the dangers of the pub and lager – he could be led astray

If your man scored 31 and over

Your man is 80% Shaftesbury Man – your only hope is to get him away from Shaftesbury and allow the lager content to reduce to 5% so that the IQ level can rise sufficiently to have a sensible conversation and, hopefully, sex!

If your man scored 80 – there is no hope I'm afraid – your man is lost to the wilderness of the pub, the lager content is beyond recovery and his morals beyond redemption – He is Shaftesbury Man!

The best revenge on the woman who steals your own Shaftesbury Man

She can keep him!

What is that insensitive bit at the base of the penis called?

Shaftesbury Man

And Finally

**Shaftesbury Man's girlfriends
may come and go**

But female enemies they accumulate!

Sorry Officer, didn't see you there